SHOW PEOPLE

BY PAUL WEITZ

★

★

DRAMATISTS
PLAY SERVICE
INC.

SHOW PEOPLE was produced by the Second Stage Theatre (Carole Rothman, Artistic Director; Timothy J. McClimon, Executive Director) in New York City, opening on March 16, 2006. It was directed by Peter Askin; the set design was by Heidi Ettinger; the costume design was by Jeff Mahshie; the lighting design was by Jeff Croiter; the original music and sound design were by Lewis Flinn; the production stage manager was Rachel J. Perlman; and the stage manager was Kit Ingui. The cast was as follows:

TOM	Ty Burrell
NATALIE	Judy Greer
MARNIE	Debra Monk
JERRY	Lawrence Pressman

CHARACTERS

TOM
NATALIE
MARNIE
JERRY

SHOW PEOPLE

ACT ONE

The living room of a large house in Montauk, Long Island. Out the window is a glimpse of the ocean, black and glimmering under a clear fall day. The front door of the house opens, and Marnie comes in. Marnie's in her sixties. Her beauty has ripened with debauch.

MARNIE. ... We're here! *(She waits.)* Weeeeeeeeeee're heeeeere. *(Jerry comes in. He is a little older than Marnie. His handsome features are sagging a bit.)*
JERRY. Hello! We are here! *(Theatrically.)* We are here ...
MARNIE. *(Forcefully.)* WE'RE HERE.
JERRY. WE AAARE HEEEEERE!
MARNIE. How do I look?
JERRY. Incredible. Me?
MARNIE. Never better. *(Marnie is shaking her arms out, breathing in and out. Jerry clears his throat theatrically. Violin music can be heard faintly. Jerry goes to the foot of the stairs.)*
JERRY. Sounds like someone left the stereo on. Hello?
MARNIE. Where is the little pervert?
JERRY. You don't know that he's a pervert. I think he's a very handsome young man.
MARNIE. He's a pervert.
JERRY. You think everyone's a pervert.
MARNIE. I'm right.
JERRY. Most people have a strange thought now and then, but that doesn't mean they're all perverts. And, if *everyone* was a pervert, wouldn't that make them all *normal?* Think about that.
MARNIE. Well you must admit, there's something abnormal about him. I mean this is abnormal, Jerry. *Abnormal.*

5

JERRY. Now Marnie, our son isn't abnormal.

MARNIE. He isn't our son.

JERRY. He is for the next three days. *(Calls out.)* Hu-looooo. *(Pause.)* Can't you understand, can't you sympathize? His happiness, his whole future lies in our hands. We've got a responsibility here.

MARNIE. How about her? How about this poor girl we're about to deceive?

JERRY. You really do look terrific. *(Jovially.)* Tom? Tommy boy, where are you? *(Marnie goes to the bar.)* Already?

MARNIE. What, "already?"

JERRY. It's early. What you ought to be doing is getting into character.

MARNIE. I'm in character, darling.

JERRY. This is a very difficult task. It's an audience of *one*. Have you ever acted for an audience of one?

MARNIE. *(Significantly.)* Yes. More often than you know.

JERRY. Oh, that's low, Marnie. That's a low blow ... I can't believe you'd drink before a performance.

MARNIE. I'm not drinking. Who's drinking?

JERRY. You're not going to let me down, are you?

MARNIE. Of course not. You know you can trust me on stage.

JERRY. I hope so.

MARNIE. When have I ever let you down?

JERRY. Opening night of *The Happiest Couple*, the Belasco Theater, October seventeenth, Nineteen Seventy Two.

MARNIE. You have to drag up this ancient history again?

JERRY. Two minutes. Two minutes I was up there on that stage waiting for you to enter. All the critics were there.

MARNIE. My dress ripped. *(Jerry is brooding.)* For Christ's sake, I changed as fast as I could.

JERRY. That was my night. I never got it back. You rattled me, and it blew my whole performance.

MARNIE. You could have ad-libbed.

JERRY. I froze.

MARNIE. Ad-lib. AD-LIB for God's sake. Or get off the stage. But you just stand there, lighting matches, and staring at the flames, like you were hypnotized. It was weird.

JERRY. They killed me. They raked me across the coals. The critics had a Burn Jerry party.

MARNIE. You were great the next night. And you weren't the only one slaughtered. The *Times* called me "frumpy, dumpy, and ill at ease in her own body."

JERRY. I wanted to kill him for that. You were regal. They just couldn't see it.

MARNIE. That play was too old-fashioned anyway. People were running around naked at the theatre down the street. Nobody wanted a comedy of manners.

JERRY. You were beautiful when you played that role.

MARNIE. Well I ain't beautiful now.

JERRY. I think you're beautiful.

MARNIE. Cut the crap.

JERRY. You are beautiful. You're a beautiful girl. *(Jerry comes over to the bar and closes the liquor cabinet.)* Isn't this a wonderful place? I think we might be in for a very fun weekend. *(Looking out.)* Heck of a view over here. Look at those waves crashing. *(Jerry hugs her.)*

MARNIE. Jerry, what's that?

JERRY. What's what?

MARNIE. Is that an erection?

JERRY. Yes, I believe it is.

MARNIE. The sea air must be affecting you.

JERRY. I'm just excited. It's wonderful, to be back on the boards again, with you at my side, just like the old days.

MARNIE. Mmm. *(Marnie turns around and kisses him warmly.)* That's all you're getting.

JERRY. Oh, look, a humidor. *(There's a beautiful wood cigar humidor on the coffee table.)*

MARNIE. Stay away from that, Jerry. You know Dr. Tarr would have a fit. *(From offstage, we hear the voice of Tom, mid-thirties.)*

TOM. MOM? DAD? *(Tom hurries in, excited. Loudly:)* You're here!

JERRY. Hulloooo!!! Tommy boy!!!

MARNIE. *(Wary.)* Good morning.

TOM. Let me look at you a second. *(He opens a cell phone, takes a picture.)* You look great. Absolutely great. Perfect.

JERRY. Thank you.

TOM. *(Quietly.)* You're a little late, I was getting worried.

MARNIE. That's because he refused to believe that Montauk is on the south fork.

JERRY. It's been a while. I forgot which fork to use.

TOM. Well I'm just glad you're here. I can't tell you how excited I am. This is going to be perfect. Natalie can't wait to meet you. I think this is going to happen.

JERRY. *(Conspiratorial.)* So, where is she?

7

TOM. Upstairs. Can't you hear her? *(They look up. The violin is still playing.)*

JERRY. Is that her? We thought it was the stereo. She's wonderful!

TOM. *(Proud.)* Yes. She's — actually, she's been having a hard time with this part of the — *(He listens to the violin playing.)* Not bad not bad, she's over the hump. Hold on, I'll — *(He starts up the stairs.)* NATALIE? *(Marnie takes Jerry aside.)*

MARNIE. *(Whispers.)* Ask him for a raise.

JERRY. What? Now?

MARNIE. Now. While we have him by the balls.

JERRY. Marnie. The young man and I made a deal. And Jerome Steel does *not* renege on a deal.

TOM. *(Returns.)* Do you two need to warm up or anything?

MARNIE. No, we're already warm.

JERRY. We're ready to go, Tom. Good to see you, *son. (Jerry gives Tom a big hug. Tom laughs.)*

TOM. *(Happily.)* Thanks, thanks, *Dad,* you too. And *Mom. (Tom tries to hug Marnie, but she backs away, air-kissing him.)*

MARNIE. Mmoi. Mmoi.

TOM. You look excellent. Well-dressed, but not showy. Can I — *(He reaches over and adjusts her scarf.)* There. Perfect. *(Tom starts up the stairs.)* NATALIE?

MARNIE. Before she comes down, there's something Jerry would like to talk about with you.

TOM. *(Nervously.)* "Jerry"?

MARNIE. I mean "Theodore."

TOM. Listen, you have to — you have to stick to the names.

JERRY. Of course we will.

TOM. Or else this whole thing is going to fall apart.

JERRY. Absolutely. *(The violin has stopped.)*

TOM. *(At the stairs, nervous.)* She's coming — is — is everything okay?

JERRY. A-Okay.

TOM. Good. I have a lot of things going on right now, I'm under a lot of pressure, I need you to perform for me. If you can't do it, then please leave right now, before she sees you.

JERRY. Can't do it? What are you talking about? Of course we can do it.

MARNIE. Can't do it? We could do it with our eyes closed.

JERRY. You won't find two better actors — you won't find two better *parents* than we are.

8

MARNIE. Sweetie, we don't have to sell ourselves. But it's true. We are good.

TOM. ... I know. I know you are.

JERRY. It's going to be fine. I guarantee by the end of the weekend she'll be *begging* to get into this family.

TOM. Good, I ... I already bought the ring.

JERRY. Terrific. *(Winks.)* It's in the bag. Right, *Estelle.*

MARNIE. ... Of course, *Theodore.*

JERRY. Now why don't you give our son a hug?

MARNIE. You give him a hug.

JERRY. I already did. Estelle, we're a warm, loving family, right?

TOM. Right.

JERRY. I think you ought to give our son a hug.

MARNIE. He doesn't want a hug. *(To Tom.)* Do you want a hug?

TOM. A hug would be good. I mean ... it would be good if Natalie saw us hugging.

MARNIE. *(Pause.)* Alright. Let's do it. Let's hug.

TOM. Thank you. Thank you very much. It's been a really long time since I just had a hug. *(Tom comes over, and Marnie and Tom hug as Natalie comes down the stairs.)*

NATALIE. Hi! You must be Mr. And Mrs. Lamont!

JERRY. You must be Natalie! *(Natalie is in her late twenties. She's well-dressed, attractive.)*

NATALIE. Have you been here long? Sorry, I was practicing.

JERRY. We know —

MARNIE. You sounded marvelous!

NATALIE. Thanks, I've been having some trouble with that piece.

TOM. Sweetheart, this is my mom —

NATALIE. I know it's your mom.

MARNIE. I'm Estelle. It's nice to meet you, dear. *(Marnie shakes her hand warmly.)*

TOM. And this is my Dad —

JERRY. *(Warmly.)* — Jerry.

TOM. *(Simultaneous.)* — Ted.

JERRY. *(Catching himself.)* Ted. Theodore Jerome Lamont. Call me Ted, or call me Jerry. Just don't call me Mr. Lamont. *(Covering.)* Well, Natalie, Tom told us you were pretty, but I had no idea you were *this* lovely.

NATALIE. *(Smiles.)* Thanks.

JERRY. *(Winks at Tom.)* Beautiful, and talented. Some fellas get all the luck. *(Jerry kisses Natalie's hand. Marnie frowns.)*

9

NATALIE. I've heard so much about the two of you! I feel like I already know you!

MARNIE. Yeeeeees, well.

NATALIE. You must be exhausted. How long a flight is it from Switzerland?

JERRY. Ten hours. Not so bad. And we had a night at the Carlyle to rest up.

MARNIE. It's good to be back. No matter where we go, New York will always be home. Although I do love London.

JERRY. London, London. She's always talking about London. What have the Brits got that we don't?

MARNIE. Talent. *(A phone rings. Tom takes out a cellular.)*

TOM. 'Scuse me. *(Into phone.)* Yes?

NATALIE. Him and his cell phone.

TOM. Un-hunh. Un-hunh.

NATALIE. I've been trying to get him to name it, you know, to humanize it a little, it's such a big part of our lives –

TOM. No, no, we don't want it in Yen, do we? Why be at the mercy of the currency market. Yeah, Listen, Hank, I — the whole EEC?

NATALIE. *(Over Tom's speech.)* Maybe Fritz, or Woodstock. Woodstock the cell phone. I gave him a yellow phone for Christmas, but he won't use it —

TOM. — Hank, listen, I can't get into this right now, we have guests. My parents. That's right, my parents. They're in from Switzerland. Sure. Soon as you find out, call me back. *(He hangs up.)* Sorry. I should really just turn the damn thing off. But I'm sort of — in the middle of something.

NATALIE. Did he tell you?

MARNIE. What?

NATALIE. He's been negotiating with Microsoft to buy his company.

TOM. We've been dancing around with them for the last few months. Microsoft's been looking to get into protective software for international banking for a while, so they think it could be a good fit if they just buy Pro-tech.

JERRY. Well that's very exciting!

TOM. My partner Hank is doing most of the negotiating, I'm sitting back, playing the bad cop. *(Jerry is looking at Tom, smiling.)* What?

JERRY. Nothing, I just … can't believe how grown up you are. *(Jerry puts his hand on Tom's shoulder, seemingly moved.)*

TOM. Wow ... thanks, Dad. *(Tom looks touched. He looks at Natalie, a bit embarrassed.)*

NATALIE. You two sure look alike.

JERRY. *(Surprised.)* Think so?

NATALIE. Well, he's — he's a combination of the two of you. He has your eyebrows, and Estelle's ... mouth.

MARNIE. So, what kind of money are we talking here? ... for your company.

TOM. It's pretty good money.

NATALIE. "Pretty good"?

TOM. Well, really good. At least to me. To them, it's nothing. *(Shrugs.)* One seven five.

JERRY. *(Considering.)* One seven five, hunh? One seven five ... one seven five what?

TOM. One hundred seventy-five million. At least that's where I'm thinking we'll end up. We're both playing hardball right now.

MARNIE. A hundred seventy-five million dollars?

TOM. You still wish I'd become a lawyer, mom?

MARNIE. No ... I wish your father had. A hundred seventy-five million dollars ... *(Pause.)* We're so proud of you, darling.

TOM. Thanks, Mom. Alright, enough talk about money. Let's show them their room, sweetie.

NATALIE. It's got a nice view of the beach.

TOM. Are your bags in your car? I'll get them. *(Pauses. Takes out his cell phone.)* Say Cheese! *(Tom takes picture of Marnie, Jerry and Natalie.)* It's just so great to have you here! *(Tom exits out the front door.)*

NATALIE. Umm, well ...

MARNIE. ... Well ...

JERRY. Welly, welly, well. *(They all stand there a moment.)* You really did sound wonderful up there. Perhaps you'll play for us later.

NATALIE. Oh, sure, I'm — my quartet is doing a concert in San Francisco in a couple of weeks. It's a very difficult program, mostly Bach. *(Pause.)* Does either of you play an instrument?

MARNIE. I used to play the accordion.

NATALIE. Really?

JERRY. Just for laughs, you know —

MARNIE. I was pretty good, actually —

JERRY. She just dabbled.

MARNIE. I love standing out in the crisp morning air in Geneva, squeezing my accordion.

11

JERRY. Just a hobby, she wasn't in a Polka band or anything —

MARNIE. No, I was out on the street with a monkey and a tin cup. *(Pause.)*

NATALIE. Well, Tom. Tom's so excited that you're visiting, he's been talking about it for weeks.

JERRY. He's a sweet boy.

NATALIE. Yes.

JERRY. A good boy. A wonderful son.

NATALIE. Can I show you your room?

MARNIE. I tell you what, dear, you go ahead. We'll be right up.

NATALIE. Okay! *(Natalie goes up the stairs.)*

JERRY. The accordion? We never said Estelle played the accordion.

MARNIE. It came to me. I was improvising. You used to love when I played the accordion.

JERRY. This isn't *us,* dear.

MARNIE. Why can't Estelle play the accordion?

JERRY. Because, the accordion is a working class instrument.

MARNIE. A "working class instrument"? Listen, Jerome Perlmutter, at least I come from good farming stock, not some den of communists on the Lower East Side. Jerry, I want a raise.

JERRY. For what? We haven't done anything yet.

MARNIE. Talk to him, Jerry. One hundred seventy-five million!

JERRY. Yes. Staggering.

MARNIE. Demand more, Jerry. More. Are we going to be suckers our whole lives?

JERRY. Look at this long-term, Marnie. Look at the big picture. We could have quite a run here, if we play our cards right. He may need parents for Christmas, for instance.

MARNIE. You've really gone bonkers, Jerry, if you think I intend to come here for Christmas.

JERRY. Why? You have other plans?

MARNIE. What do you mean, do I have other plans? We'll be going to Bernie and Ellen's, of course.

JERRY. You think so, after the stunt you pulled last year?

MARNIE. It was a joke, for crying out loud.

JERRY. You pulled his pants down in front of the whole party.

MARNIE. Everyone had a good laugh.

JERRY. Everyone was mortified. Mortified. *(Tom comes in, struggling with a heavy suitcase, as well as a couple of lighter ones. Jovially:)* Tom-O!

MARNIE. *(Whispers.)* A raise, Jerry. *(Calling up the stairs.)*

Coming, Natalie! *(Marnie exits up the stairs, leaving Jerry with Tom.)*

JERRY. Sorry about that. She always overpacks. She must have six pairs of shoes in there. Here, let me get that big one.

TOM. That's alright, I've got it. *(Tom hangs onto the heavier bag, letting Jerry take a much smaller one.)*

JERRY. Nice place. Must have cost a fortune.

TOM. Yeah, it did.

JERRY. She's lovely, Natalie. You make a great couple.

TOM. *(Pleased.)* You think so?

JERRY. Sure, sure, I have an intuition about these things. I'm seldom wrong.

TOM. *(Happy.)* Really?

JERRY. And it's not always the most obvious couple who are meant for each other. People said my wife and I wouldn't last more than a month.

TOM. Oh. Well … *(Tom struggles towards the stairs.)*

JERRY. Um, Tom — could I talk to you for a second?

TOM. Sure.

JERRY. Tom-O, I'm aware that you and I have an agreement. And we're delighted to be here, we both are, really, so I hope you won't misinterpret this …

TOM. *(Worried.)* Wait — *(Looks up the stairs.)* I thought Natalie was coming. What? Misinterpret what?

JERRY. Well, you see …

TOM. Yes? Can we talk about this later?

JERRY. Absolutely. We'll have time to chat later. Now, did you like that business with my hand, that gesture —

TOM. What gesture?

JERRY. This one. *(Jerry makes an open gesture with his hand.)* I think it's subtle, but I'm looking for gestures, little bits of business, to show what kind of an open, sharing guy this character is. Did you notice it?

TOM. No, I'll look for it.

JERRY. Good. I don't want to go too big with it. I really like this character. *(They both pick up their bags and head up the stairs. Lights up on the living room as we hear the pop of a champagne bottle being opened. Tom is standing by the bar, where he puts the champagne into some ice. He brings four champagne glasses over to the coffee table, setting them carefully. Then he lifts over the ice bucket. He looks at the scene for a moment, and decides the ice bucket was better over by the bar, so he hauls it back … Natalie comes in from the kitchen, wearing an apron.)*

13

TOM. They're great, aren't they? My parents?

NATALIE. And they're so proud of you.

TOM. *(Pleased.)* Yeah …

NATALIE. Especially your Dad.

TOM. Dad's — dad's a great guy. We've always had a special thing. A bond.

NATALIE. And your mom's lovely.

TOM. Thanks. Thanks.

NATALIE. I just hope they like me. They're a little intimidating.

TOM. Come on, I'm sure they like you. You're beautiful, you're smart. They're happy for me.

NATALIE. Really? Well that's … that's good.

TOM. I used to find my Dad intimidating. He had a real, a real temper. Nothing violent, except sometimes. But that was a long time ago. *(He smiles.)* Are you cooking something?

NATALIE. Baking. I'm baking blueberry muffins.

TOM. Blueberry muffins? Why?

NATALIE. I thought people might like some.

TOM. Blueberry muffins. *(Considers this.)* Well, sure. Why not? Home-made blueberry muffins. Sounds great. I was going to open some caviar, but it can wait.

NATALIE. Oh, right, the caviar. Well, look, we can forget the muffins.

TOM. No, no, it's good to improvise. Let's go with the muffins. Muffins it is. *(They look up as Jerry and Marnie come down the stairs.)*

JERRY. Something smells delicious!

TOM. Natalie's been baking!

JERRY. Baking? You play violin, you bake, is there anything you can't do?

MARNIE. No, she's perfect.

TOM. Remember those pecan pies you used to make, Mom?

MARNIE. The ones with pecans?

TOM. I used to love her pecan pies.

JERRY. She wouldn't let me touch them. "Those are for Tommy!"

MARNIE. You two have some memory.

NATALIE. Well I love baking. Ever since I was a kid, I've had sort of a talent for it.

JERRY. Your parents are scientists, aren't they?

NATALIE. Dad's a physicist.

TOM. He's not just *a* physicist.

NATALIE. *(Shrugs.)* He has his own research lab. My mom was a diplomat, and now she teaches political science.

MARNIE. They sound fascinating.

JERRY. We look forward to meeting them someday. You'll have to arrange it, Tom-O!

MARNIE. Now Theodore, I'm sure they're very busy people.

TOM. I think it would be great if everyone met. I'm sure you'd all get along. *(Pause.)*

MARNIE. O-kay. *(Pause.)* Oh look, champagne. Grand Dame. My namesake.

TOM. I thought we might have a glass of champagne before going to dinner. I made a reservation at the Lobster House. The food's not bad. *(Tom takes the champagne out of the silver champagne bucket.)* Do you like the champagne glasses?

JERRY. Sure.

TOM. You should, you gave them to me, remember?

JERRY. Right!

NATALIE. I'd better check on the muffins.

TOM. Can I pour you some champagne, sweetie?

NATALIE. Champagne? No. Well, yes, a little. Why not? *(Tom smiles as Natalie goes into the kitchen.)*

TOM. Champagne? Mom? Dad?

MARNIE. I suppose I might have a glass —

JERRY. *(Simultaneously.)* Oh I don't think so, it's still early.

MARNIE. What are you talking about? It's 6:30.

JERRY. We'll have a drink after dinner.

TOM. Oh come on, Dad, have a little champagne. We have some caviar too.

JERRY. Caviar? What kind?

TOM. Beluga, from Petrossian.

JERRY. Beluga ... from Petrossian ...

TOM. I think it's from the last two remaining sturgeon in the Caspian Sea. But Natalie started baking so ...

JERRY. I see, I see ...

MARNIE. Well, I'd love a glass.

TOM. Coming right up.

JERRY. If there's caviar, a little ... champagne and caviar might be refreshing. *(Natalie comes in from the kitchen holding a tray with about ten muffins on it.)*

NATALIE. Muffins!

JERRY. Oh, wonderful.

TOM. Here, Nat. *(Tom hands Natalie a glass of champagne. She takes a little swig and sets the glass aside.)*

NATALIE. Plates! *(Natalie rushes back into the kitchen.)*

MARNIE. She's a whirlwind.

TOM. Well, she loves to bake. *(Natalie comes back in with some plates.)*

NATALIE. Would everyone like one?

TOM. Of course, sweetie. *(Tom smiles as Natalie holds the tray for them.)*

NATALIE. I hope you like them.

TOM. I'm sure they will. *(They taste their muffins. Natalie is watching closely.)* Mmm, wonderful.

JERRY. Delicious.

MARNIE. Marvelous. *(They all put the rest of their muffins down on their plates. They're still chewing.)*

TOM. *(Chewing.)* Nice texture.

JERRY. *(Chewing.)* Chewy … in a good way.

MARNIE. Delicious. Simply delicious. *(She pauses, and then takes another bite.)*

NATALIE. They're not too sweet, are they?

TOM. No, they're … a little salty, actually. Is there … horse radish in them?

NATALIE. A dash. I do them two ways. Sweet for kids, and not so sweet for adults.

JERRY. Well these are not so sweet.

MARNIE. They're sort of tangy.

NATALIE. Most people think of muffins as a breakfast thing, but why not have them for dinner?

JERRY. Well by goodness, they're good. They might even go well with caviar.

TOM. Okay, dad, I'll open the caviar.

MARNIE. Don't give him any caviar until he's finished his muffin.

NATALIE. *(Anxious.)* You don't like them, do you?

TOM. Are you kidding? They're great. I'm having two.

JERRY. Two? *(Pleased, Natalie gives Tom a second muffin.)*

TOM. I'd like to make a toast. To the three most important people in my life. Thank you for being here, mom and dad. And thank you, sweetheart, for baking these muffins. For filling my life with music. And for being so wonderful and supportive to me all the time. *(Tom drinks to Natalie.)*

NATALIE. Gosh, that's — that's so sweet!

JERRY. Here here. That's what it's all about. *(Tom's phone rings.)*

TOM. Damn. *(Answers.)* Hello? Hi, Hank. What's up? *(Pause.)* Un-hunh? Un-hunh. No kidding. Well they're bluffing. How do I know? I know. Just remember, they came after us. Not vice versa. Listen, I'll — I'll call you back in a second, Hank. Yes. Call you right back. *(He hangs up.)* I've got to take this call. I'm sorry, I shouldn't be talking business now, it's just bad timing. I won't be long. Sorry.

JERRY. It's alright, I can open the —

TOM. Back in a second. *(Tom goes off up the stairs. The three of them sit there awkwardly for a moment.)*

NATALIE. He's — he's such a sweetheart. *(Pause.)* Your son's a gem, really. I hope you know that.

JERRY. Well, of course we do.

MARNIE. Oh, sure.

NATALIE. Good, because, he really loves you. *(Natalie takes the remaining muffins into the kitchen.)*

JERRY. I guess we'll have the caviar later.

MARNIE. Would you quit it with the caviar?

JERRY. Quit what?

MARNIE. The girl just baked us some muffins with her own bare hands, and all you can talk about is caviar.

JERRY. Really?

MARNIE. Who cares if the damn things were inedible. She put a lot of effort into it. She wants to please us, Jerry. Can't you see that?

JERRY. You're right. You know, she doesn't seem the judgmental type. I expected a real snob from what Tom said.

MARNIE. She's a lovely girl.

JERRY. You're right, Marnie, you're right. *(He kisses Marnie on the forehead.)* You're a good joe, Marnie. A good egg. *(Marnie smiles. Jerry gets up and goes to the kitchen door.)* Natalie? I tell you what, I'll have another muffin.

NATALIE. *(Offstage.)* You will? *(Natalie comes back in with the plate of muffins.)*

JERRY. I'll just take this small one.

MARNIE. Come on in and sit down, dear. Stop rushing around.

NATALIE. … Alright.

MARNIE. Have a little more champagne. *(Marnie tops up Natalie's glass, which was half full.)*

NATALIE. I really shouldn't. Champagne goes right to my head.

MARNIE. It's the bubbles. They make the alcohol rise. *(To Jerry.)* Darling?

JERRY. Okay. What the heck. *(Marnie pours Jerry some champagne.*

Then she puts the bottle down.)

NATALIE. Can I pour you some?

MARNIE. *(For Jerry's sake.)* That's alright, I think I'll just nurse this for the moment.

NATALIE. *(Sipping.)* Nice champagne.

MARNIE. It's my favorite, actually.

JERRY. It's thoughtful of Tommy to remember his mother's favorite champagne. But Estelle taught Tommy from an early age to be considerate to others. Every Thanksgiving, the two of them would make a turkey together, and then carry it over to the church to feed the homeless.

NATALIE. That's — that's wonderful.

JERRY. And every Christmas, she took Tommy and his classmates out caroling.

MARNIE. Now dear, let's not overdo it.

NATALIE. Tom's lucky to have parents like you. I mean you … you seem like such warm people.

JERRY. Well, we love our boy. *(He prods Marnie with a hug.)*

MARNIE. Love, love, love.

JERRY. We're lucky to have Tom as a son. And we're especially lucky that he has the good sense to meet up with a beautiful, smart, young woman like you.

NATALIE. Thank you. You're so kind.

JERRY. Natalie, I've only known you for a short while. But I have a sense about things like this. And I think you and Tom are perfect for each other. You're certainly wonderful for him. I can see it in his eyes.

MARNIE. And we hope Tom's good for you, too.

NATALIE. Tom's wonderful. He's generous, and … he's a gentleman. You should be very proud.

MARNIE. It's very important to know the other person well.

JERRY. They know each other, dear, they've been living together for …

NATALIE. … eight months …

JERRY. Eight months —

MARNIE. I'm just saying it's important to be aware of the other person's little … quirks.

JERRY. Where love blooms, everything else falls into place.

NATALIE. I wonder where Tom is —

JERRY. Natalie, I hope you don't think I'm being too intrusive. But I can honestly say that … I hope someday we can welcome you into our family.

NATALIE. *(Moved.)* Thank you.

JERRY. It took Tom a long time to find the right, special person to be with. But now I see that he has. And seeing it makes me happier than you can know.

NATALIE. — Thank you —

JERRY. In fact, to be completely honest with you, I've always wanted to have a daughter. And if I were ever to have a daughter … well … *(Lifts his glass.)* A toast! To Natalie. We're so happy to be here with you. Estelle?

MARNIE. *(With sympathy.)* Best of luck, Natalie.

NATALIE. Wait. *(Jerry and Marnie pause before drinking.)* Don't — don't drink to me. *(Pause.)* I can't go through with this any more. You're such wonderful people, and you're being so kind to me. *(Sets aside her glass.)* This is a terrible thing to tell you, and it's going to be a big shock, but … I haven't been living with Tom for eight months. *(Pause.)* And I'm not really a violinist. That was just a recording you were listening to. *(Pause.)* You see I'm not really Tom's girlfriend.

JERRY. Excuse me?

NATALIE. I'm an actress. *(Pause.)* I'm just an actress. I don't really belong in your lives. I'm — I'm so ashamed. *(Natalie puts her hands over her face. Marnie breaks into cackling laughter.)*

MARNIE. I'll be damned. What do you think of *that?*

JERRY. What can I say? I'm shocked.

NATALIE. I don't mean to betray Tom. He's been so nice to me. But I can't go on with this charade anymore. Try and understand. He was only trying to please you. I—I never would have told you this, but you seem like such wonderful people, such loving parents, I just can't keep lying to you. And I don't think he should either. Mr. and Mrs. Lamont, your son is gay.

MARNIE. Really? Hear that? He's gay!

JERRY. You're kidding. He doesn't seem gay.

MARNIE. What'd I say, Jerry, he's a grade-A pervert.

NATALIE. *(Upset.)* Please, don't call him that! He's your child! I know this whole thing comes as a shock, but — if you could find it in your hearts to accept him … He's your son. What does it matter if he's straight or gay?

MARNIE. Listen kid, I don't care if he's straight, gay, or Catholic. We only met the man three weeks ago.

NATALIE. Met which man?

MARNIE. Tom.

NATALIE. I'm sorry, I don't understand.

JERRY. We're also actors.

NATALIE. Excuse me?

MARNIE. We're actors. We're not his parents. We've been hired to play them for the weekend.

NATALIE. What? *(Pause.)* But that's — that's bizarre.

MARNIE. Jerry here doesn't think so. Jerry think it's all hunky-dory.

NATALIE. Jerry, so — your name is Jerry.

MARNIE. I'm Marnie Todd. And this is my husband, Jerome Steel. We were once actors. We were both on Broadway. And Jerry here had his own television show, which shot in Europe, called *Spy Man*.

JERRY. We shot eighteen and a half episodes.

MARNIE. And what's your real name?

NATALIE. My real name is Natalie. Natalie Henning.

MARNIE. Why'd *she* get to use her real name?

NATALIE. I'm sorry, so — so — you're not really his parents?

MARNIE. No.

JERRY. He told us his real parents abandoned him. He was ashamed of them. So, he'd lied to his girlfriend, saying he had these wonderful parents who lived in Switzerland.

MARNIE. Et voila. Instant parents.

NATALIE. But … you seemed like such a wonderful father.

JERRY. Thank you. So you believed me in the role.

NATALIE. I wanted you to be *my* father.

JERRY. I tried to portray Ted as someone who wasn't afraid of showing emotion, but at the same time was rock solid and strong. There aren't enough good parents out there nowadays.

NATALIE. Well you were … you were great.

JERRY. *(Pleased.)* Thank you. Thank you.

MARNIE. Too bad the *Times* wasn't here. *(Pours herself some champagne.)* Jerry, go look at the caviar. If it hasn't been opened yet, stuff it into your pocket. *(She drains her glass.)* At least the champagne was real. *(She gets up.)* Natalie, it was nice meeting you. Good luck in all your future endeavors.

JERRY. Are you going somewhere?

MARNIE. Come on, Jerry. Stop fooling around. If we haul ass, maybe we could get home before midnight.

JERRY. You really want to drive all night now? We just got here!

NATALIE. I don't understand. Why would Tom do this? *(Marnie does a circling motion at her temple and whistles like a loon.)*

MARNIE. Because he's nuts.

JERRY. We don't know that. He may just be eccentric.

MARNIE. Jerry, eccentric is wearing a bolo-tie. This, on the other hand, is nuts. Now let's get going. I don't want to have to stay at a motel. I'm not spending another cent on this craziness.

JERRY. But that's just it, Marnie. We don't have to spend anything. In fact, we can still get *paid* a good sum, if we don't let on that we've all had this conversation.

MARNIE. Be realistic, will you Jerry, for once in your life?

JERRY. I *am* being realistic. You're the one who's overreacting. I mean what has changed, really? We've all been hired to do a role, and we can still *do* it. The only thing is, we can't let *him* know that we know that *she* knows.

MARNIE. Welcome to Jerry's world. It's a nice place to visit …

JERRY. *You're* the one who's being emotional this time. I've got my eye on the ball. Don't you want to be paid?

MARNIE. Jerry, this man is *disturbed*. For all we know he's going to walk down those stairs holding an axe.

JERRY. Oh come on, Tom's not violent.

MARNIE. "Tom's not violent." How do you know his name's really Tom?

JERRY. You've got a point. But I do know he's not violent. I've been around violent people.

MARNIE. When?

JERRY. When I did *Chain Gang Harry*, I spent a day in a maximum security prison doing character research. A violent person gets a look in his eyes. You can't hide it, it's … *(Jerry does the look.)* Tom doesn't have this look.

MARNIE. Well you look like a chimpanzee.

JERRY. What we should all do is go back into character. Let's be professional here. We're actors. Let's act.

MARNIE. If this is acting, Jerry, where's the script?

JERRY. Up here. *(Jerry points to his head. And then to his heart.)* And in here.

MARNIE. I tell you what. I'll leave it up to a vote.

JERRY. That's right. You haven't told us your opinion, Natalie. Do you think we should run out of here like a bunch of wimps?

NATALIE. Well … *(Natalie thinks.)* I see both your points. I don't feel very comfortable here. But I don't think Tom's dangerous. But how can we tell? I mean they said Ted Bundy seemed like a really sweet guy, right? But I feel sort of better now that I know you're just actors too. Less guilty. But I'd like to know why he's doing this.

What does he want from us? But I need the money. I really need the money.

MARNIE. Well, God knows, so do we. *(Pause.)* How much are you getting paid anyway?

NATALIE. … Thirty thousand.

MARNIE. *Thirty thousand!*

JERRY. Marnie, Ssssh!

MARNIE. Don't shush me, Jerome Steel. Did you hear that? Thirty!

NATALIE. He offered me ten, but I talked him up.

MARNIE. Christ. I wish you'd negotiated *our* deal.

NATALIE. Why, what are you getting?

MARNIE. A lousy ten grand, for the both of us.

JERRY. It seemed good at the time. I'm an artist, not a business-man.

MARNIE. Well you're certainly not a businessman. You still want to stay?

JERRY. I do. Even more so! Now we have inside information. I'll reopen negotiations! So Natalie, what's the verdict? Are we staying or going?

NATALIE. Don't make me decide — I hate making decisions —

MARNIE. Fine, I'll make it.

JERRY. We're actors, Natalie. And I think you're doing a wonderful characterization.

NATALIE. Really?

TOM. *(Offstage.)* Sorry, everyone! *(Tom comes down the stairs, looking happy.)* Sorry it took so long, but it's going great! *(For a moment they all just look at him.)* The deal. They're caving in! I'm bringing Microsoft to its knees! Now I'm going for the jugular. Natalie, I never would have been able to do this without you. Mom and Dad, I have to tell you, Natalie has been so supportive throughout this whole thing. There are so many times I would come home from work, and I was so drained, and down, and depressed. But you … *(He looks at Natalie, moved.)* You would talk to me, and bring me out of my funk, and tell me I was special. That I had something to offer. And you'd make me laugh. I take myself so seriously some-times. I'm such a pain in the butt. I'm self-important, and moody, I think the whole world revolves around me. To be honest, I don't know why you put up with me, Natalie. But I just thank my lucky stars that I came to Michelle's party that night and met you. It was the luckiest night of my life. *(Natalie doesn't reply.)* Natalie, umm

... I'm about to do something terrible.

MARNIE. No, don't!

TOM. *(Looking up.)* Don't what?

MARNIE. Don't do anything terrible.

TOM. Mom, I'm just — I just want to give Natalie this. *(Tom takes a small velvet box out of his pocket.)* I know it's awful to do this in front of my parents, but ... I hope you'll forgive me because ... well, it seems like ... everything in my life is coming together this weekend. *(Looks at Jerry and Marnie.)* My past, and ... *(Looks at Natalie.)* My future, I hope. Natalie, you're so kind and smart and beautiful and real. Natalie ... *(Tom takes a ring out of the box. Tom gets down on his knees before Natalie.)* Natalie, my love ... will you marry me? *(Everyone looks at Natalie. A long pause. Natalie looks up at Jerry and Marnie, who await her decision.)*

NATALIE. *(Pause.)* Yes. Yes, I will. *(Jerry smiles, while Marnie's shoulders slump.)*

TOM. You will?

NATALIE. Yes.

JERRY. Good choice!

MARNIE. *(Quietly.)* Now we're in for it.

TOM. *(Swept up in emotion.)* Natalie, you've made me the happiest person on earth. *(Tom puts the ring on Natalie's finger. She stares at the big sparkler.)*

NATALIE. *(Impressed.)* It's beautiful. It's a beautiful ring.

JERRY. Well this deserves a celebration.

TOM. Everyone, I just want to say, this is the most perfect day of my life ... *(Blackout.)*

End of Act One

ACT TWO

Tom and Marnie and Jerry and Natalie are coming in from dinner. Tom hangs up their coats for them.

TOM. You know, maybe having the wedding in Switzerland isn't such a bad idea after all! *(To Jerry and Marnie.)* We can have it at your house, can't we? *(To Natalie.)* It's magnificent, we'd say our vows looking out over the alps!

JERRY. Well, that's — that's an interesting idea, Tom-o. Just when would this be?

TOM. What do you think, sweetheart? Next spring? Is that too soon?

NATALIE. Spring. Spring sounds wonderful.

JERRY. Spring in Switzerland's okay with me.

TOM. What do you think, Mom?

MARNIE. Oh sure, Switzerland. I'll be there. Right on top of the alps.

NATALIE. Of course, right here might be nice. We could do the ceremony out on the beach.

TOM. That's a nice idea, Natalie. Very romantic, don't you think, Dad?

JERRY. Well, sure, but Switzerland —

TOM. — I still think at least three-hundred guests.

MARNIE. Now that could get expensive.

NATALIE. Why so many people? A nice, intimate wedding would be better. Maybe … fifty people. Just family, and a few friends. That way it's really a special experience for everyone.

TOM. Natalie, You're right. You're absolutely right.

NATALIE. I don't want a totally conventional ceremony. We'll write our own vows, right?

TOM. Sure. Absolutely. It will be perfect, because it will come from the heart. It'll be simple, pure and honest. Not like all those big crappy commercial weddings.

NATALIE. I was at a wedding once where these Tibetan monks rang a gong.

JERRY. Well I think some of these weddings nowadays are very

24

strange. People getting married in tree houses. Eighty-year-old women marrying seventeen-year-old men. You know, some people even have their pets get married.

MARNIE. He still manages to get *The National Enquirer*, even in Switzerland.

TOM. I just want us to be happy. That's all I want. We could get married in a clerk's office somewhere. As long as I was marrying Natalie, it would be the most romantic place I'd ever been in my life.

NATALIE. That's so sweet.

TOM. Dad, I've been thinking … I've got a lot of friends, but … I really don't feel like I have a better friend than you. I'd like you to be my best man.

JERRY. I think every father dreams that someday his son will say something like that to him. Sure, Tom-O, I'd be honored. *(Tom smiles. They embrace.)*

MARNIE. Who am I going to sit with? *(Pause.)* Oh, what does it matter. *(Mutters.)* Listen to me. "Who am I going to sit with?"

TOM. Hey, you can be my best man, too! You and Dad can both be my best men.

NATALIE. That's a little weird. I mean — both your parents standing up there with you?

TOM. You said you wanted to be unconventional.

MARNIE. Forget it. I'll be fine. I'll amuse myself somehow. I'll bring some cards, maybe. So, anyone want a nightcap? What have we got here? *(She goes to the liquor cabinet.)* Cognac … *(Pulling out a bottle.)* Ah, the Macallan.

JERRY. Estelle, it's been such a long day —

MARNIE. Single malt revives me.

TOM. I hope you're not too tired, Dad, because I had a really fun idea, I thought we could all play Scrabble and drink hot cider, like when I was little.

MARNIE. Is the hot cider mandatory?

JERRY. Dear, a little hot cider's not going to kill you.

NATALIE. My Dad used to get angry when he lost at Scrabble. He'd claim I was cheating, then he'd toss the board in the air, send the letters flying everywhere.

MARNIE. He sounds like a shit.

TOM. *Mom* —

NATALIE. No, he is sort of a shit.

TOM. But sweetie, he's a world-renowned physicist.

NATALIE. He is that, yes.

TOM. I'll get the board, okay?

JERRY. Okay, Tom-O! *(Tom goes off up stairs.)*

NATALIE. Is this really happening?

MARNIE. No.

JERRY. I think we all feel that way about our wedding: "Is this really happening?" we ask ... is this me? Is that her? Is that my bride?

MARNIE. You sound like Frankenstein.

JERRY. I'm just saying there's an element of the surreal to the whole thing.

MARNIE. I know I felt that way, because we were married on the stage of the Lunt Theatre.

NATALIE. So you two were really on *Broadway?* That's incredible.

MARNIE. What's so incredible about it?

NATALIE. What plays were you in?

JERRY. Oh, *The Laughing Man. He Who Stoops. Slap Happy.*

MARNIE. We called it *Crap Happy.*

NATALIE. And you acted together sometimes?

MARNIE. All the time. In fact he proposed to me during the fourth act of *The Wild Duck* in Boston. I'll never forget. He was playing Hjalmar, I was Gina. And he said —

JERRY. "Tell me — don't you every day, every hour regret this spider web of deception you've spun around me? Answer me that? Don't you really go around in a torment of remorse?"

MARNIE. He had worked himself around so his back was to the audience —

JERRY. And I opened a velvet box with a ring inside it, so only she could see —

MARNIE. And he whispered "Will you marry me?" And I said out loud "Yes, Hjalmar!"

NATALIE. How romantic ... and unprofessional.

JERRY. Touring Ibsen can get very tiring. You have to do something to break up the routine. *(Pause.)* Of course my big claim to fame was my TV show, *Spy Man.* We shot it in Europe, I starred, and wrote and directed a few episodes.

NATALIE. Wow. Never heard of it.

MARNIE. Don't worry, nobody has.

JERRY. Some people have.

MARNIE. Darling, no one. No one.

JERRY. Some people have. Fans. Aficionados. I'm told there's a lot of chatter about it on the internet.

MARNIE. No, that's Al Qaeda, Jerry.

JERRY. Ladies, could you please, please get your heads in these roles? The two of you are leaving me floundering out there. Natalie, you're acting very strange —

NATALIE. Strange?

JERRY. Carving a heart out of butter at the dinner table? I call that strange.

NATALIE. *(Concerned.)* You don't think I'm doing a good job?

MARNIE. What does he know? *(Finishing her drink.)* I think she's *smashing.*

NATALIE. *(Excited.)* Do you really? I'm just trying to bring some real stuff to it. It's a little disturbing; I think he's the nicest guy I've ever been involved with. You know, I'm not sure he's really gay. He kept staring at me over his lobster.

MARNIE. I am a little curious: Are you supposed to sleep with him tonight? Is that part of the thirty thousand?

NATALIE. No, of course not.

MARNIE. *(Disappointed.)* Oh.

JERRY. And you, Marnie, you're just being terrible. Ordering two lobsters and just eating the tails.

MARNIE. The rest of the lobster is too damn much work.

JERRY. And ordering Dom Perignon, at a restaurant!

MARNIE. Why not? Why shouldn't I live it up for once? I haven't had champagne in years.

JERRY. — Natalie, you have to stay within the confines of the character. Did he *tell* you the character was into ... Tibetan gonging?

NATALIE. Well, no, but I am —

JERRY. It doesn't matter if you are. Stick to the character. And Marnie, if this is your idea of how an affectionate mother would act —

MARNIE. He always thinks he's the director!

JERRY. Is this how you would have acted with our kid? *(Pause.)*

MARNIE. *(Icily.)* No, Jerry. This isn't how I would have acted with our kid. *(Pause.)*

JERRY. ... I know. I know that, Marnie.

MARNIE. How dare you? Jerome Steel. How dare you?

JERRY. Marnie, I'm — I'm sorry — it was a stupid thing to say.

MARNIE. It's so typical of you, Jerry. Here you are, more concerned with this creature, this *audience* up there, than with your own wife. I'm your *wife,* Jerry. This isn't pretend. We actually have to go *home* together. Our only audience there is the dog. This guy is *stiffing* us. Don't you understand that? A lousy ten grand. Theatre tickets cost ten grand nowadays. Who's looking out for us, Jerry? Who's taking care of the situation?

JERRY. That's not fair — I've always provided for the two of us.

MARNIE. Jerry, you can't even provide Alpo for our *dog*.

TOM. Here we go, Scrabble! *(They all jump a little. Tom comes down the stairs, holding the Scrabble set.)*

TOM. Scrabble time!

JERRY. Terrific. *(A bit weakly.)* This is fun, remember those after-dinner games of Scrabble, with the hot cocoa —

MARNIE. Hot cider. Get it straight.

TOM. Speaking of which, I've got some cider, so we can heat it up. Sweetheart, would you mind?

NATALIE. Oh. Sure. *(Natalie goes into the kitchen. Tom's phone rings.)*

TOM. Hello? Look, I can't talk now, Hank. I'm with my family. No, I don't care, I don't want to hear it. My family comes first. We can leave it alone for one night. No. No. No. No. *Good night*, Hank. *(He hangs up.)* There, hope he got the message.

MARNIE. I have a headache.

TOM. *(Concerned.)* Can I get you an aspirin?

MARNIE. That's alright, I have some in my bag. Will you excuse me?

JERRY. Are you okay, Estelle? Estelle?

MARNIE. Go to hell, Theodore. *(Marnie exits up the stairs. Tom looks at Jerry. Jerry smiles a little sheepishly.)*

TOM. Is Mom angry about something?

JERRY. Oh no, no.

TOM. But she told you to go to hell.

JERRY. That's nothing. Just an expression. More or less affection-ate. Possibly less.

TOM. I've never heard Mom swear like that.

JERRY. Uh Tom, believe me, that's — that's nothing.

TOM. We're still going to play Scrabble, aren't we? *(Natalie comes back in.)*

NATALIE. Okay, I've got the cider warming up.

TOM. Good.

NATALIE. Where's Estelle?

JERRY. She went up to get an aspirin. *(Tom starts laying out the board. Natalie goes up the stairs.)*

TOM. Wait a minute, where are you going?

NATALIE. I thought I'd see how Estelle's doing. I'll be right back down.

TOM. Oh. Oh, alright. But hurry up. Scrabble. *(Natalie goes off up the stairs. Jerry and Tom are left alone.)* We're so lucky, aren't we?

JERRY. Lucky?

TOM. You've got Mom, and I've got Natalie ...

JERRY. Oh, yes.

TOM. A lot of people go their whole lives without finding someone they're compatible with.

JERRY. I suppose that's true.

TOM. That's why I feel so lucky to have Natalie. She's so beautiful, and substantial. She has depth.

JERRY. Well, you know women, they're ... much smarter than men.

TOM. This is the only time I've ever felt this way about a woman. The only time I've really felt comfortable and secure in a relationship. I've always had a hard time being myself around women. And around men.

JERRY. That pretty much covers it.

TOM. I think I'm not very likeable. I've always had a likeability problem. You remember, the kids. How they used to scare me.

JERRY. Bullies, you mean?

TOM. Oh, not just the bullies. The other kids too. They'd lock me in the broom closet at school, or pull my pants off while I was in the bathroom.

JERRY. Well that's — that's terrible.

TOM. *(Shrugs.)* You know how kids are. Anyway, I wonder where they all are now, hunh?

JERRY. Well, they're ... probably not as successful as you.

TOM. Probably not. They're probably nowhere. And I'm here. I've made it.

JERRY. You have, Tom.

TOM. And now I'm starting on a new life, with Natalie.

JERRY. Well ... Congratulations.

TOM. But it's really because of your example. You and Mom. You showed me what it was like to have a successful, loving relationship.

JERRY. Well, uh ...

TOM. To have a relationship like you and Mom have ... to stick with each other through thick and thin ... to honor the wedding vows, to always be faithful to each other ...

JERRY. *(Glancing upstairs.)* Mmm ...

TOM. It's inspiring. It really is. How do you do it?

JERRY. Do what?

TOM. Stay so in love with each other?

JERRY. *(Pause.)* Well, she's ... look, my wife and I, we're ... we've been together a long time. A long, long time. Since she was an ingenue. And ... when you're with someone that long, it's like the tide on a rocky shore. The waves crash against the rock, and ... after years and years, they shape the rock. The rock gets shaped a certain way, and it's not going to go back to its old shape. You have to live with what it's turned into.

TOM. Un-hunh ...

JERRY. You're a young man. You have your life ahead of you ... Marnie ... she is my life. She's ingrained in me. I met her when we were both aspiring young actors, fresh in New York, I mean ... I came from the Lower East Side, my father was in the Yiddish the-ater, you see, but Marnie, well she comes from Missouri. *Missouri,* by God. Who'd ever heard of Missouri? But she was the most beau-tiful, and ... the most talented young woman I'd ever met. And I wanted ... I wanted to be with her for the rest of my life. I want-ed to make a home with her, and ... take care of her. I've done a pretty mediocre job of it, if I'm to be honest with myself. *(Jerry looks up at Tom.)* I'm sorry. The point is, Tom, maybe it's good that we have a chance to talk for a minute.

TOM. I think it is good. It's great that we're bonding.

JERRY. I feel like we *are* bonding, in some strange way.

TOM. I'd like to get the others down here. It would be nice for Natalie to see us bonding like this.

JERRY. Hey, what's the hurry? How about some of that cider? *(Lights down on them, lights up on Marnie and Jerry's room. Marnie is sitting with a washrag over her eyes as there's a knock on the door. Natalie comes in.)*

NATALIE. Am I interrupting anything? *(Marnie gives her a look, then puts the washrag over her forehead.)* Do you mind if I ask you a question?

MARNIE. What?

NATALIE. Do you think I'm a good actress?

MARNIE. How am I supposed to know?

NATALIE. I came to New York six years ago to be an actress, and ... this year, my only role was I played a topless horse in an avant-garde play based on Picasso's *Guernica.*

MARNIE. A topless horse?

NATALIE. I mean, I was topless, in the role. The director talked me into it. He wanted me to do it completely nude, but I drew the line.

30

MARNIE. It's important to have standards.

NATALIE. So I'm prancing around on stage with my boobs hanging out, snorting and kicking, when I see my stepfather in the audience. He hasn't seen me act since the first grade. He never came to any of the high-school musicals. But he was in New York for the weekend for a Toyota sales convention. And he decided to surprise me by coming to my play, because I sent my mother a postcard about it. Now he's sitting in an audience of ten people, who are outnumbered by the actors, and I've got my tits exposed, I'm neighing, making a complete idiot of myself. And the worst thing was, after the performance, he told me he never knew I had that much talent.

MARNIE. Would you mind passing me a glass of water? *(Marnie points to a water jug, which Natalie pours for her.)*

NATALIE. So anyway, after the stepfather thing I decided that was it, I was going to quit acting and go back to Columbus, and start a muffin business called "Magnificent Muffins." I've always liked baking, and … look at Mrs. Fields. But the only thing is … I've tasted Mrs. Fields, I like Mrs. Fields and … I'm no Mrs. Fields.

MARNIE. No. You're more like a prison cook.

NATALIE. You're an actress. I mean a real actress. You've been on Broadway. In straight plays. *(Handing Marnie a glass of water.)* You're like some magnificent dinosaur.

MARNIE. How nicely you put it.

NATALIE. The stage is your home.

MARNIE. Yes. I've been homeless for a few years now.

NATALIE. You see you've … you've lived my dream. I mean I guess you're … not doing so well financially, or you wouldn't be here. And maybe you have a problem with alcohol, and maybe you're bitter about how your career and your life have gone, but so what? At least you've lived on the stage. I'd go through all that and more just to be a real actress.

MARNIE. Have you read *The Seagull*?

NATALIE. No, I haven't.

MARNIE. I think perhaps you should. Thanks for the visit, kid.

NATALIE. Do you not like me?

MARNIE. I'm on the fence.

NATALIE. Good. That'll make this easier.

MARNIE. What?

NATALIE. I want to do a monologue for you. And then I want you to tell me whether you think I'm a real actress or not.

MARNIE. No. I refuse to listen to a monologue.

NATALIE. You have to.

MARNIE. Why?

NATALIE. Because this weekend — I knew this weekend was going to change me, change the course of my life … Here, I'll give you this. *(She takes off her ring.)* I'll give you this if you'll listen to my monologue.

MARNIE. I don't need any more costume jewelry.

NATALIE. Maybe it's not costume. I mean he's crazy, right? Maybe he's crazy enough to give me a real diamond.

MARNIE. Let me see. *(Marnie inspects the ring.)* I can't tell. It's the story of my life.

NATALIE. It could be worth thousands. If it's real.

MARNIE. It's not real.

NATALIE. What if it is?

MARNIE. It's not. *(Pause.)* Is it a *long* monologue?

NATALIE. Not too long.

MARNIE. … Alright. Let's hear it.

NATALIE. Good. I want you to be totally honest with me.

MARNIE. Okay. *(Shrugs.)*

NATALIE. You do understand what I'm saying is I'm going to do a monologue for you and based on your reaction, I'm either going to stick it out in New York, or I'm going to move back to Ohio.

MARNIE. I get it.

NATALIE. I just want you to take this seriously. Clear your mind and focus.

MARNIE. *(Laughs.)* You think the audience is going to clear its mind and focus? Maybe, if you're lucky. But more likely you're going to have to focus it for them. You see they're sitting out there, and maybe they're thinking about what you're saying. But just as likely they're wishing they hadn't ordered the calamari for dinner. And they're wondering how long the second act is, and whether the guy playing the butler is wearing a toupee, and what would he look like naked? What it would look like if they were all naked, having an orgy. You see, you're going to have to transcend the vulgarity, the vulgarity of everyday experience, in fact the vulgarity of theatre itself, in order to make your point. If you think you can do that, be my guest. Do your monologue. But if you're expecting sympathy take it somewhere else. I gave at the office, sister.

NATALIE. Fair enough. I still want to do it. *(Pause. Natalie concentrates quietly for a moment. Then she looks up at Marnie, in character.)* To be, or not to be — that is the question.

MARNIE. Time out.

NATALIE. — What?

MARNIE. You're doing Hamlet for me? *(Natalie nods.)* You're aware that Hamlet's a man?

NATALIE. Yes. I'm aware.

MARNIE. Just checking.

NATALIE. But I can relate to him. I've wanted to kill my stepfather before … this is my classical piece, I could do Sam Shepard instead.

MARNIE. Go ahead with Hamlet.

NATALIE. Alright … *(She collects herself again.)* To be, or not to be. That is the question. Whether 'tis nobler in the mind to suffer the slings and arrows of outrageous fortune or to take arms against a sea of troubles and by opposing end them. To die, to sleep — No more — and by a sleep to say we end the heartache and the thousand natural shocks that flesh is heir to … *(Lights fade down on them. They fade up on Jerry and Tom, downstairs. The Scrabble game is laid out, and they both have cider.)*

JERRY. You see, Tom, I'm … I'm not a wealthy man. I'm not a businessman, I'm an artist. Well, now I wish I'd been a little bit more of a businessman. Tom, frankly, I'm broke.

TOM. *(Laughs.)* You're not broke.

JERRY. I'm broke.

TOM. How can you be broke?

JERRY. It's easy. You just … don't have a job for ten years. Look, not that — not that this is your problem —

TOM. But what about all your investments? I thought they made you enough income to last the rest of your life.

JERRY. My investments? Tom, the only investment I have is a lottery ticket I bought yesterday.

TOM. Look, just — tell me what you need, Dad. I owe you so much. Without you and Mom being such wonderful parents, I never would have been able to make it.

JERRY. *(Pause.)* Tom, I've uh — you know I've … *(Jerry glances around.)* … Stepped out of character here for a moment. We're backstage, so to speak —

TOM. Look, I'm serious, whatever you need, you don't have to worry about it, because I'm going to take care of it. I mean … you in particular. Of all people, I've always felt I could *count on you.* Because in this world, in this world, the only thing you can be sure of is that you can't rely on anyone — except to kick you, and humiliate you, any chance they get.

JERRY. Well, that's … an exaggeration. Look, I — I more than most people know what it's like to be kicked around. That's what acting is — it's rejection. And when you get old, and no one knows who you are, or what you've done, it takes it to a new level. I mean it's as if the whole thing, your whole career, all you worked for, was a dream. But to say that the world is out to get you — no, you can't think like that. That's egocentrism, Tom.

TOM. No, it's not. It's the truth. And I'm not blaming anyone. I've looked at the world. And I've looked at myself. And from where I stand, I deserve it. I deserve to be stepped on.

JERRY. No you don't. No one does.

TOM. Well … of course you say that. You're my Dad. *(Tom's phone rings.)* … Dad, why don't you tell Natalie and Mom to come back down.

JERRY. Uh, Tom I — I'm not sure you understand what I've been getting at here. What I'm saying is, it's time for me to take some more responsibility … *(The phone is still ringing.)*

TOM. Hang on …

JERRY. … to — to stop being above it all. You see ten thousand in my day was a large amount, but it's not my day anymore, is it?

TOM. Dad, I'm sorry, hold on — *(He answers the phone.)* Yes? Hank, I told you I was — He what? *(Tom looks shocked.)* Excuse me?

JERRY. I'm not talking about a very large sum here, Tom, but if you could sweeten the deal to —

TOM. *(Into phone.)* Whoa, whoa, slow down. This is — this is coming out of nowhere, is this — are you serious? I mean do you think they're serious?

JERRY. Thirty thousand dollars, Tom. Thirty thousand dollars is nothing to you.

TOM. Dad, please. *(He walks away with the phone.)* Now look, look, you know their program is nowhere near as advanced as ours. We all know that.

JERRY. I've been thinking about it Tom, and … it's right to give us more. Because you can afford it, and —

TOM. *(Into phone.)* Since when have they been talking to Samuelsson?

JERRY. Do you think you could — could you put down the phone for a moment?

TOM. *(Cupping into phone.)* Dad, this is business, okay?

JERRY. I'm talking business too, Tom.

TOM. What? Hold on. *Hank.* Hank, this isn't clean, this isn't fair negotiating tactics. Yes, I know it's Microsoft.

JERRY. Tom —

TOM. *(Walking away.)* Hank, tell them it's unacceptable. No, absolutely not, I won't fly to Seattle tomorrow.

JERRY. Tom-O —

TOM. Yes, that's my final word. We have to be strong here, Hank. Call their bluff.

JERRY. Tom-O —

TOM. *(To Jerry.)* Would you please shut up! *(Into phone.)* No, not you. Call me back, Hank. Call me as soon as you've talked to them. *(Tom hangs up.)* Stop calling me "Tom-O"! You know that bothers me.

JERRY. Oh … It does … well, I just — you see my Dad used to call me "Jerr-O," so — silly. Listen, I'm — I'm talking to you about a raise.

TOM. *(Pause.)* A raise.

JERRY. Tom, I'm … in need. I have a wife, and a dog. My wife hasn't bought a new dress in longer than I can remember. And she's a beautiful woman. She was when I married her, and she is now. A beautiful woman needs some new clothes every now and then. Tom, I'm sorry, I know we had an agreement, but … please, could you raise us to thirty thousand?

TOM. You need thirty thousand dollars?

JERRY. Yes.

TOM. *(Pause.)* Well, fine. Listen, if you have a liquidity problem, just say so. *(Tom picks up the phone. Hits redial.)* Hank. No, I know. Listen, I want you to do something for me. I want you to FedEx me a cashier's check for thirty thousand dollars. Make it out to cash. *(Pause.)* Yes. *(Pause.)* It doesn't matter why. I want you to do it. Thank you. Yeah. Call me when you hear anything. *(He hangs up.)*

JERRY. That's it? He's — he's going to send it?

TOM. It'll be here first thing on Monday morning.

JERRY. Tom, this is wonderful. I can't thank you enough.

TOM. It's nothing.

JERRY. *(Goes to stairs.)* I'll just go see what's keeping the ladies so long. I'll be right back down, and we can all have a nice family evening!

TOM. Dad? *(Jerry stops.)* I love you.

JERRY. Okay! *(Jerry hurries upstairs, leaving Tom alone downstairs. Tom sits there, with a blank expression on his face … Lights down on*

him, and up on Marnie and Natalie. Marnie is sitting at a small desk.)
MARNIE. You have to commit.
NATALIE. I'm committed. I think I am.
MARNIE. You need to remove the distance between the character and you.
NATALIE. What does that mean?
MARNIE. What does it mean … what does it mean … I think what it means is that … unlike real life, the stage is a place that demands empathy. You have to empathize with the character. Empathize with your fellow actors. Even empathize with the audience, the poor bastards. And to do this, you must first STOP BEING SELF-CONSCIOUS. So try again. And this time don't think. And whatever you do — don't act!
NATALIE. Don't act … don't act … you know, you should be a teacher!
MARNIE. I've thought of it. Jerry and I were offered once, a decade ago, but he wouldn't hear of it. He thinks teaching is the last step before the grave.
NATALIE. Well … couldn't you just do it? I mean … why did you always act with your husband?
MARNIE. You don't want to pry open that nut too hard … but … when it was good … being onstage with him was like really great sex that lasted for two hours. And then you got applauded at the end of it. And also … I just liked being around the son of a bitch. *(Pause.)* Thanks for asking. So let's try that monologue again.
NATALIE. Alright …
MARNIE. Don't act.
NATALIE. For who would bear the whips and scorns of time, Th' oppressor's wrong, the proud man's contumely, the pangs of despised love, the law's delay, the insolence of office — *(Jerry comes in.)*
JERRY. *(Happy.)* Marnie —
NATALIE. — And the spurns that patient merit of th' unworthy takes —
JERRY. What's going on here?
MARNIE. Hamlet, Jerry.
NATALIE. — When he himself might his quietus make with a bare bodkin? Who would fardels bare —
JERRY. I know it's Hamlet.
MARNIE. Next she'll be doing Stanley Kowalski. *(Jerry joins in, reciting the speech along with Natalie.)*
NATALIE and JERRY. — to grunt and sweat under a weary life,

36

but that the dread of something after death, the undiscovered country, from whose bourn no traveler returns, puzzles the will, and makes us rather bear those ills we have than fly to others that we know not of? *(Jerry takes over.)*

JERRY. *(With gusto.)* Thus conscience does make cowards of us all! And thus the native hue of resolution is sicklied o'er with the pale cast of thought, and enterprises of great pitch and moment with this regard their currents turn awry and lose the name of action, soft you now, the fair Ophelia! *(Leaping towards Marnie.)* Nymph! In thy orisons be all my sins remembered.

MARNIE. What's gotten into *you?*

JERRY. *(Excited.)* Marnie, I did it!

MARNIE. What did you do now, Jerry?

JERRY. I got the money! I got our raise: thirty thousand!

MARNIE. How?

JERRY. I asked! I wouldn't take no for an answer!

MARNIE. You're not pulling my leg, are you?

JERRY. It's coming Monday morning. By FedEx.

MARNIE. That's great. Great Jerry. *(She gives him a big kiss.)* I'm proud of you.

NATALIE. Congratulations!

MARNIE. *(To Natalie.)* Keep working.

JERRY. Marnie, we — mmm — *(They're kissing.)* We have to get downstairs, or we could blow it all.

NATALIE. *(To Marnie.)* Start from the top?

MARNIE. No, we'd better take a break. We'll get back to it later.

NATALIE. We'll work more later?

MARNIE. Yes. Come on, Natalie. Get your butt in gear. *(Getting up.)* You know, I could get used to this gig!

NATALIE. I need my ring!

MARNIE. Good. Now remember, stay focused. This is the happiest night of your life.

NATALIE. Happy, happy, happy …

JERRY. All together now. We're going to nail this!

MARNIE. Scrabble time! *(Lights down on them, up on the living room, where Tom is sitting alone, holding his cell-phone. Natalie, Jerry and Marnie come downstairs.)* We're back!

JERRY. Hey there, Tomeroonie, look who I found!

NATALIE. She's feeling a lot better.

MARNIE. I'm even willing to play Scrabble. Of course I'm functionally illiterate, so you'll have to allow alternative spellings.

NATALIE. I've got an idea. Why don't we play charades?

JERRY. Now *there's* an idea. Tommy, you used to love charades when you were a little boy.

TOM. Did I?

JERRY. Sure you did.

TOM. Okay. Let's play charades.

JERRY. Great!

MARNIE. I haven't played charades in years.

JERRY. I've got one. *(He holds up three fingers.)*

NATALIE. Three words ... A play. *(Jerry waits. Looks upstage left. Waits.)*

MARNIE. Waiting — *Waiting for Godot.*

JERRY. Right. Your turn. *(Marnie holds up two fingers.)*

NATALIE. Two words. A musical. *(Marnie acts like a vampire biting a victim.)*

NATALIE. Umm ... you're a vampire ... sucking blood ... *Dracula!* That's not two words —

JERRY. *The Producers!*

MARNIE. Right! *(Off Jerry's gestures.)* A play — seven words — fourth word — *(Jerry mimes searching.)*

NATALIE. Looking ... you're looking, seeing —

MARNIE. — searching — *Six Characters in Search of a Play!* *(Marnie signals.)*

NATALIE. A play. Three words. Third word. *(Marnie mimes a celebration.)* Celebration. A parade. Drunk.

JERRY. *The Birthday Party!*

NATALIE. This is spooky!

TOM. It's over.

NATALIE. What, Tom?

TOM. It's over. *(They look at him.)*

JERRY. What's over, Tom?

TOM. I got a call from Hank. Microsoft is buying another company. They've stopped negotiating with us. *(Pause.)* They were using me all along. I was a decoy. They really wanted to buy one of my competitors. They were just using me to drive the price down. *(Pause.)* I leveraged everything. I was counting on this sale going through.

MARNIE. So what does this mean?

NATALIE. You still have money, don't you?

MARNIE. To be more specific, you still have thirty thousand dollars?

TOM. Mom, everything I have, I owe to the banks ... This house

... the Mercedes ... it's all mortgaged ...

JERRY. But you have your business.

TOM. We're running in the red. And now Microsoft is going to crush us. *(Pause.)* I'm ruined. Mom? Dad? I'm ruined. *(Tom puts his head in his hands.)*

JERRY. Listen, Tom. I'm sure you're not ... ruined ... you don't go from being a success one day to being a failure the next.

MARNIE. Why not? We did.

TOM. What am I going to do? What am I going to do?

MARNIE. Alright, here's what we do. Tomorrow morning, we go down to a used car lot, and sell that Mercedes you have in the driveway for however much cash we can get.

NATALIE. Umm, we can sell the diamond!

TOM. Sell the diamond? Natalie ... *(Tom holds out his hand to Natalie.)* Natalie, this doesn't change anything between us, does it?

NATALIE. Uh —

TOM. Natalie? I — I need you.

NATALIE. Tom, umm ... you really have no money?

TOM. What difference does that make? Natalie, you're not just with me for my money, are you?

NATALIE. *(Pause.)* Well ... no, umm of course, I mean, you're a great guy, don't get me wrong —

TOM. I'm a "great guy"? Wow. Wow. Mom? Dad? You'll support me, won't you? I know you hate failure, mom, you used to cry if I got below an A minus in school, and dad, you always used to say life's a war. You said I was too much of a coward to succeed. But I'll get back on top, I will! *(Tom starts to cry.)* You don't love me. None of you loves me.

MARNIE. Jerry. Deal with this.

JERRY. How?

TOM. Mom, you never loved me. I don't even think you're capable of love. You're cold. You're a cold person. You were never meant to be a mother.

MARNIE. Excuse me? Listen, chum, one thing I am capable of is a swift kick in the pants!

TOM. Fine. Hit me. I thought it would be different now, that after all these years, things would have changed. But it never does. The way you were drinking at dinner, it reminded me so much of my childhood. Those embarrassing scenes. Like that New Year's Eve when you set the Christmas tree on fire.

MARNIE. What the hell are you talking about?

TOM. That New Year's Eve party, where you got drunk and nearly burned the house down.

MARNIE. Odd how I don't remember this.

JERRY. I think I do, vaguely.

MARNIE. *(Disgusted.) What?!*

JERRY. Well, I remember something *like* it.

TOM. *(To Jerry.)* And it was something *you'd* done that set it off.

MARNIE. Now I'm remembering!

TOM. *(Still to Jerry.)* You disappeared at the party with my cousin Nancy. Did — did something happen with you and Nancy?

MARNIE. He's onto you, Jerry.

TOM. *(To Marnie.)* I've always just been a burden to you, an embarrassment. Well SCREW YOU, MOM!

JERRY. Tom, I think you need to calm down here —

TOM. And you ... did you actually enjoy it? Did you enjoy wailing on me with your belt?

JERRY. Excuse me? I never would hit a child, I love children —

TOM. With parents like you, I guess it's no surprise that I ended up with Natalie.

MARNIE. There's nothing wrong with Natalie.

NATALIE. Thank you.

TOM. Emotionally, Mom, emotionally she's frigid.

NATALIE. I am not frigid! I'm just a little detached!

TOM. You don't really love me!

NATALIE. I just met you! And you're insane!

TOM. You're a user! A manipulator!

NATALIE. I don't have to put up with this! I'm going to leave. I don't care about the money. I'm leaving.

TOM. You see, she *admits* she's with me for my money! *(Natalie tries to hand him back the engagement ring.)*

NATALIE. Here, take this.

MARNIE. Uh, wait a second, I'll take it —

JERRY. Tom, I'm very disappointed in you. There's no call for this kind of craziness.

TOM. I just want to know one thing, Dad. Why did the two of you ever get married? You don't love each other. In fact, you make each other sick. *(Marnie rears on him.)*

MARNIE. Now listen here, you little bastard. You think you had a hard time having *us* as parents? Well try having *you* for a son! *(They all look at Marnie, surprised.)* You were a sullen little creature, from the day you were born. No, *before* that. Do you know the *hours* we spent reading to you while you were in the womb? We read you poetry. Yeats. Rilke — in the original German! We read you *Robert Frost,* dammit! And I *hate* Robert Frost. I went through a *twenty-three hour* labor with you, you were so reluctant to face the world, it was like giving birth to a mule! And when you finally *did* emerge, I've never seen a less lovable baby. You never smiled, never laughed. You used to cry, wail at the top of your lungs, until one of us came rushing in at four in the morning, then you'd stop crying immediately, and you'd stare at us, with this unpleasant, critical expression on your face. You know what your first word was?

TOM. Dada?

MARNIE. No. We just *told* you it was Dada. But really, it was *"Mine!"* You used to sit there in your crib, saying "Mine! Mine! Mine! Mine!" You were an *ugly* baby. And a bully. We couldn't put you in a crib with another child, because you'd pinch them. But *still* we loved you.

JERRY. *(Trying to stop her.)* Don't —

MARNIE. Your father was so proud. His face beamed when he was around you. You could *feel* his heart swelling up with love for his son. It was something he wanted his whole life. A *child.* We tried, and tried, had our hopes raised up and dashed, so many times, and finally, just when we'd given up hope, *you* arrived.

JERRY. — Sweetheart …

MARNIE. You arrived, and you broke our hearts. Well, you know what, I'm *glad* we never had children. I'm glad, Jerry. Because *this* is how they end up!

JERRY. … Marnie … *(He goes to her.)* Marnie … *(He puts his arms around her.)* Marnie, I'm sorry … I'm sorry for this insanity … I don't know what I was thinking. We'll leave right now.

TOM. I'm sorry, too. *(Pause.)* Mom, please forgive me. *(Pause.)* Dad, you understand. I'm sorry, Dad. I didn't mean the things I said.

JERRY. I'm not your Dad.

TOM. Dad, I love you —

JERRY. I'm not your Dad.

TOM. Dad, please, I need you —

JERRY. Tom … I'm an actor. I'm not your father. You hired me. You hired all of us.

TOM. What are you talking about?

JERRY. It's over. I don't want this anymore. I'm an actor. We're all actors. *(Pause.)* You're not my child. We never had a child. *(To Marnie.)* We never had a child.

41

TOM. ... Alright. I see. I understand. *(Tom takes a key out of his pocket.)* My business has fallen apart ... *(Tom unlocks the cigar box.)* My fiancée is leaving me ... *(He takes a pistol out of the humidor.)*

MARNIE. Oh my God —

TOM. And my own parents ... my own parents are turning their backs on me. *(They watch, frozen.)*

NATALIE. No —

JERRY. Tom, don't — *(Jerry takes a step towards him.)*

TOM. Get back! *(Tom backs away, pointing the pistol at his heart.)*

NATALIE. Tom, you're freaking me out!

JERRY. Wait! Hand me the gun!

TOM. Get back! You gave me something to live for and now it's over.

JERRY. Tom! Tom! Don't! *(Tom backs up into the corridor, offstage. Jerry follows him — There is a BANG.)* NO!

MARNIE. Holy God!

NATALIE. *(Shrieks.)* AAAAA! *(Jerry shrinks away from Tom. Then he steps forward, offstage for a moment.)*

MARNIE. *(Grimacing.)* Jerry — Jerry, did he —

JERRY. Yes ... *(He comes back onstage.)* Yes, he did. *(Natalie starts to cry. Jerry takes Marnie gently, steers her away from the corridor.)* In the heart, Marnie. Don't look.

MARNIE. Is he ...

JERRY. His eyes are open. He's staring, Marnie. He's staring ... *(Jerry crumples.)* I'll never be able to erase it from my mind! It's the most horrifying thing I've ever seen!

NATALIE. It's my fault!

MARNIE. What? Why is it your fault?

NATALIE. Because ... he liked me. He maybe even loved me. And I called him insane!

MARNIE. Well Jesus Christ, he *was* insane! We have to ... we have to call the police ...

JERRY. We turned our backs on him, Marnie. He was a troubled, troubled man, and he wanted something from us. He wanted us to be his family.

MARNIE. ... *You're* going to drive *me* insane!!! He was a maniac! And now we probably won't ever get paid!

JERRY. You're thinking of money, Marnie? At a time like this? *(Looks at his hands.)* We have blood on our hands. Blood, Marnie. Like ...

MARNIE. Don't say it.

JERRY. Like ... the Scottish play. And we will never ... never be able to wash it off. *(Applause is heard from offstage. They all look up as Tom enters from the corridor, clapping his hands.)*

TOM. Oh my God. Bravo! Bravo!

NATALIE. *(Screams.)* Tom! *(Tom has a large red stain on his shirt.)*

JERRY. You — you're alive!

NATALIE. We have to — we have to call an ambulance!

TOM. That's not necessary. Everything's okay. In fact everything's *great!* You were all so great.

JERRY. How — how could you survive that?

MARNIE. Jerry, you twit, he didn't shoot himself!

JERRY. He didn't?

MARNIE. Clearly.

TOM. She's right. It was a blank. And a blood squib.

JERRY. Why the hell would you do that? *(Yells.)* WHY THE HELL WOULD YOU DO THAT, YOU FUCKING MANIAC?!

TOM. You probably want an explanation.

MARNIE. I just want to take my money and leave!

TOM. I wish you could. I really do. But … I'm afraid it's not possible.

MARNIE. Why not?

TOM. Because, well, I have no money.

MARNIE. You have that Mercedes out there.

TOM. It's rented. Like the house. I maxed out my credit cards. I'm broke.

NATALIE. … Because of Microsoft?

TOM. No. Microsoft doesn't exist. I mean it does exist, but it wasn't going to buy my software company. I don't have a software company. "Hank" is a ten-year-old kid who lives in my building. I gave him five dollars to call me at random times throughout the day. The ring's a fake, too. *(To Natalie.)* I wish I could have given you a real one. You deserve it.

NATALIE. Umm … thank you?

TOM. But I don't have any money, because I spent it all, all of my savings on this production.

JERRY. … What production?

TOM. The one we all just collaborated on.

NATALIE. I'm sorry … are you saying …

TOM. … Yes …

NATALIE. … That we're in a movie?

TOM. No.

NATALIE. A TV show? Are we being punked? *(Natalie looks*

around for a camera.)

JERRY. What? "Punked"? What the hell are you talking about?

TOM. This isn't a movie. This isn't a TV show. This is so much more pure than that. So much more real. It's … it's a play.

NATALIE. This isn't a play. I've been to plays before. And this wasn't a play.

TOM. Why wasn't it?

JERRY. Why? Because a play has A SCRIPT! And AN AUDIENCE! WHERE'S THE AUDIENCE?! WHERE'S THE SCRIPT?!

TOM. Listen to yourself. A play has a script? Have you been to the theatre lately? A play has an audience? Well Jerry, we had the best audience of all. Oh, sure, we didn't have a bunch of depressed look-ing people sitting in the dark, but who cares! You know it finally dawned on me with my last production. It was a verse adaptation of *Waiting for Lefty*, with a cast of all homeless actors. I invited all the critics. But they were busy covering a musical version of *Mrs. Doubtfire*, and an evening of one acts based on David Mamet's essays on screenwriting. And I invited my usual group of "friends," who I cultivate primarily so they will attend my plays. My col-leagues from the office where I sell accidental death and dismember-ment insurance. I even invited my parents. But they won't talk to me anymore. Not until I quit the arts. They say it's "tough love." No one came. So there I was, looking out at a completely empty house — not one of the twenty seats was filled. I felt like throwing up. But instead, I went to my cast, and said "follow me." And they followed me, to the subway, and we performed the show on the six-train.

JERRY. How was it received?

TOM. Not well. I ended up getting arrested by a transit cop. But I've been locked up before, so it didn't bother me so much. And it freed me, the experience freed me. It made me think about my life. What I could have been, what I might have become if I'd followed the path my parents wanted me to. I could have been rich, maybe. I could have had a wife. My parents might have loved me. I might even have been happy. But thank God I didn't fall into that trap. Because this production, my last production, has made everything worthwhile. It's brought my life full circle. To work with you two. Because I saw you. I saw you onstage when I was a child. That's why I cast you in this.

MARNIE. You did?

TOM. My mother took me to a Broadway play. We couldn't get tickets to *Grease*, so we got half-priced tickets to your show. Turned

44

out it was opening night. It made such an impression on me. I actually kept the program. It was about a man who falls in love with his fiancée's maid of honor.

JERRY. *The Happiest Couple.* You saw *The Happiest Couple?*

TOM. There was this incredible moment when you were up on stage, Jerry, you were all alone up there, for the longest time. Not saying anything. And the audience was shifting in their seats. People started to cough. And you just stood up there lighting matches. Lighting matches and staring at them until they burned down to your fingertips. You were like God up there, making everyone beneath you squirm. The image is burned into my mind. Sometimes I've wondered whether it even really happened.

JERRY. It happened. But it wasn't like being God. It was the single worst moment in my career. Until now.

TOM. Well, it … it affected me. I think it made me want to go into the theatre.

JERRY. I guess … if it affected you … that's all I was ever trying to do.

MARNIE. For Jerry there's no such thing as a backhanded compliment.

TOM. Anyway, that's why I chose you. I googled you two and found your web-site.

MARNIE. Great idea with the web site, Jerry.

NATALIE. So why did you choose me?

TOM. You? You gave the best audition.

NATALIE. Were there a lot of people who auditioned?

TOM. I got over nine-hundred responses to my ad in *Backstage.* I auditioned forty.

NATALIE. And I was the best.

TOM. Your girl next door naivete complemented my worldly sophistication.

NATALIE. You thought I was the girl next door?

TOM. Aren't you?

NATALIE. … Yes. Yes, I am.

TOM. Also, of course, you were beautiful.

NATALIE. Hunh. *(She goes over and kisses him. Then she slaps him.)* YOU LYING BASTARD! *(To Marnie.)* You see? I can commit.

MARNIE. Right. That's wonderful.

NATALIE. So are you, or are you not gay?

TOM. I have to confess I'm not. I tried, Lord knows I tried, but it just wouldn't stick. But I had to tell you something, I needed a

45

back-story. Anyway, I want to thank all of you. I'm sorry I had to go to that dark place towards the end there, I don't — I don't think you're frigid, and … sorry about the stuff about you being a terrible mother, that was all my baggage, it just came bubbling up, and I had to go with it, it makes such a difference, working with real actors, and, I want to say, I love you all very much. And I'm sorry … *(He starts to cry.)* I'm sorry I can't pay you! I'm sorry — I'm sorry I'm worthless — I'm a worthless piece of shit — a worthless loser — I'm scum! *(Tom buries his face in his hands, groaning. Tom crying.)* I don't belong anywhere … I want to die …

JERRY. Tom, you mustn't say that.

TOM. Why not?

JERRY. … Because. *(Pause.)* Because you belong *here.*

TOM. In Montauk? *(Beat.)*

JERRY. No … In the theatre. *(Pause.)* Marnie … Tell him.

MARNIE. Where's our money!

JERRY. Marnie. Not now. Tell him.

MARNIE. Tell him what?

JERRY. You know what.

MARNIE. Must I?

JERRY. Find it in your heart, Marnie. It's there. I know it is.

MARNIE. … Alright … It was an interesting performance …

TOM. Really?

MARNIE. Really. You do belong here.

NATALIE. Do I belong here?

MARNIE. Sure. You belong here. We all belong here.

JERRY. Come on, old boy. Get up. We're leaving. We'll drive you into the city, and we'll get you some help. *(Pause.)* Now come on, be a good boy and go change your clothes.

TOM. *(Gets up.)* And … you'll be here? You'll still be here when I come back down?

JERRY. Of course.

TOM. … Alright. I'm going to go get changed. And you don't hate me because I can't pay you?

JERRY. We'll talk about it. Not now.

TOM. Okay. And you'll be here? *(Tom exits.)*

MARNIE. What a day. Now all I want is to drop this lunatic off, and then trudge up the five flights of stairs to our apartment, turn off the lights, fall down into bed … and have you fuck the living hell out of me. Think you can do that for me, Jerry?

JERRY. Sure. Sounds like a plan.

NATALIE. Umm … I'm still here.

MARNIE. I know honey. I just thought I'd show you how it's done. *(Turns to her.)* Now go get your stuff, and we'll rendezvous down here in a minute. *(Natalie nods.)*

NATALIE. Umm … I just want to say … it's been the highlight of my professional career, to have worked with the two of you.

MARNIE. Thank you.

JERRY. Yes. Thanks. *(Natalie leaves. Marnie turns to Jerry.)*

MARNIE. We'd better pack too.

JERRY. Yes. Let's. Marnie? *(She stops. Slowly, Jerry bows towards her. She bows towards him. They start up the stairs. Fade to black.)*

End of Play

ALTERNATIVE ENDING

The following alternative ending is offered in case anyone would like to present a more mysterioso production.

JERRY. It's over. I don't want this anymore. I'm an actor. We're all actors. *(Pause.)* You're not my child. We never had a child. *(To Marnie.)* We never had a child.

TOM. ... Alright. If that's how you want it. *(Tom takes a key out of his pocket.)* My business has fallen apart ... *(Tom unlocks the cigar box.)* My fiancée is leaving me ... *(He takes a pistol out of the humidor.)*

MARNIE. Oh my God —

TOM. And my own parents ... my own parents are turning their backs on me. *(They watch, frozen.)* I don't have anything to live for.

NATALIE. No —

JERRY. Tom, don't — *(Jerry takes a step towards him.)*

TOM. Get back! *(Tom points the pistol at his heart. About to shoot:)* I love you all very much.

JERRY. Please, wait — oh — oh — *(Jerry falters, clutching his chest.)*

MARNIE. *(Afraid.)* JERRY! *(Jerry falls to the ground. Tom lowers his gun.)*

TOM. Dad? Are you alright?

NATALIE. He's having a heart attack!

JERRY. *(In pain.)* Marnie — The rest is silence. *(Jerry gasps, then slumps.)*

TOM. No! *(Tom drops his gun and runs over. As he kneels beside Jerry, Marnie goes behind him and picks up the gun.)*

TOM. Is — is he okay?

NATALIE. *(Starting to cry.)* I think he's dead!

TOM. Dead? *(Marnie looks at the gun, as Tom and Natalie kneel over Jerry.)* I — I killed him. I —

MARNIE. I've got the gun, Jerry!

JERRY. Good! *(Tom and Natalie jump back.)*

MARNIE. And it's fake!

JERRY. *(Sitting up.)* What?!

MARNIE. The gun's fake, Jerry! A prop! It's got blanks!

JERRY. I'll be damned. It's a fake?

TOM. But — But —

NATALIE. You're alright? *(Jerry gets up, brushing himself off.)*

JERRY. Sure I'm alright. *(Tom slumps back into a chair and groans.)*

MARNIE. Not a bad death scene, Jerry. Relatively restrained.

JERRY. Thanks.

NATALIE. You were faking? *(To Marnie.)* But how did you know?

MARNIE. He quoted the last line from Hamlet's death scene: "The rest is silence."

JERRY. Best I could do off the top of my head.

MARNIE. Look! *(A red stain is beginning to spread across Tom's shirt. Natalie gives a gasp.)*

JERRY. It's fake. Fake blood. *(Tom looks down at his chest. Then he pulls out a packet of red liquid from inside his shirt.)*

TOM. I'm dead. *(Pause.)* You see? I'm dead. You can go now. You're supposed to go. The show is over. You are afraid, so you all grab your things and leave. You just saw a man shoot himself in the heart. It overwhelms you. You call the police from town. But when they arrive, the body has disappeared. The end.

JERRY. But why? Why?

TOM. Dad, you know why. *(Pause.)* It's because I love you. I love all of you. You're the only people in the world I've ever loved.

JERRY. You're insane.

TOM. No, I'm not. I'm no more insane than you are. In fact, we're just like each other. We're family. *(Lights dim to black. When the lights rise, Jerry, Marnie and Natalie are standing in the living room with a policeman. Tom is not onstage.)*

POLICEMAN. He made a confession. Well, I'm not sure it's a confession, because I don't exactly know what he'll be charged with.

MARNIE. Yes?

POLICEMAN. Well, first off, this isn't his house. He rented it for the weekend. He also rented the Mercedes. And I guess he told you he had a business?

NATALIE. A software company.

POLICEMAN. He lied. He's an insurance salesman. He's been unemployed for the last eight months. But he had a job selling accidental death and dismemberment insurance for State Farm.

JERRY. And "Hank?"

POLICEMAN. Hank?

MARNIE. His partner. Who kept calling him on his cellphone. *(The policeman shrugs.)*

POLICEMAN. I don't know. Maybe he paid someone to call him.

His real name's not Tom Lamont. It's David Foster.

MARNIE. Hardly worth changing.

POLICEMAN. He was divorced a couple of years ago. He says he's broke. He borrowed money to pay for the weekend. He got champagne, he said? Anyway, I guess the plan was to … pretend to commit suicide. And then leave without paying you the money he promised.

MARNIE. Umm … there was a ring.

POLICEMAN. Yeah, it's fake. Cubic Zirconium.

NATALIE. I knew it. *(They look up. Tom is at the top of the stairs.)*

POLICEMAN. Sir, I told you to wait for me.

TOM. I'm an insurance executive. I sell accidental death and dis-memberment insurance.

POLICEMAN. Yes, you said that.

TOM. Who are you people?

POLICEMAN. I'm Officer Kramer.

TOM. A policeman. Excellent. Who are the rest of these people?

POLICEMAN. You know who they are. At least you did ten min-utes ago.

TOM. They're a father, a mother, and a fiancée.

POLICEMAN. Right. Okay, we're all going to go down to the sta-tion. I'm going to put these handcuffs on you. Alright? This is for your own safety.

TOM. *(Comes down stairs.)* Of course. *(The policeman puts a pair of handcuffs on him.)*

POLICEMAN. *(To Jerry, Marnie and Natalie.)* I'd like you to fol-low me down to the station, okay?

JERRY. Yes, officer.

NATALIE. Okay.

POLICEMAN. You can talk to the desk officer. Explain the whole thing to him.

JERRY. We'll try.

POLICEMAN. I do have one question. Why? Why would you folks agree to do this?

NATALIE. We needed the money.

POLICEMAN. Yeah? Well, I can understand that.

JERRY. That's not why I did it. Only my reason, I don't think you'll understand.

POLICEMAN. Well. *(To Tom.)* Let's go.

TOM. I'll be happy to.

NATALIE. *Streetcar Named Desire.*

POLICEMAN. Excuse me?

NATALIE. This reminds me a little of *Streetcar Named Desire*. The last scene, where they come to take Blanche to the asylum.

POLICEMAN. "I've always relied on the kindness of strangers."

NATALIE. You saw the movie.

POLICEMAN. Actually, I acted in the play. Community theatre.

MARNIE. But you are a policeman.

POLICEMAN. Yeah, I'm a policeman. Of course.

JERRY. We'll follow you, officer.

NATALIE. I'll just grab my bag. Tom? *(She pauses. Takes off the ring.)* Here's your ring back.

TOM. No, keep it. It looks beautiful on you.

NATALIE. ... Alright. What the hell. Souvenir, right? *(Natalie heads up the stairs to get her bag.)*

POLICEMAN. *(Nods.)* Alright, sir. Let's go. *(As the policeman heads out the front door with Tom, Marnie goes into the kitchen. She comes out again holding a jar of caviar.)*

MARNIE. Here, Jerry. Here's your caviar.

JERRY. Oh. *(He looks at it.)* Well, at least this is real.

MARNIE. Jerry ...

JERRY. Yes? *(Marnie takes his hand.)*

JERRY. ... Marnie ... I'm sorry ...

MARNIE. For what? We have nothing to be sorry for. *(She kisses him. They kiss, gently. Natalie comes down the stairs, with her suitcase.)* We'd better get our bags too, Jerry. *(Jerry nods. They go up the stairs. Natalie looks up towards them, upstaging herself, as Marnie and Jerry exit grandly up the stairs. Blackout.)*

End of Play

NOTE: With this ending, the following beat should be inserted when Tom is helping Jerry bring their bags into the house.

JERRY. So, you're a cigar fan.

TOM. A cigar fan?

JERRY. I saw the humidor. I'm a cigar fan too. Not supposed to have 'em, though. I recently had a — you know.

TOM. A what?

JERRY. Heart attack.

TOM. A heart attack?

JERRY. Well, not recently. Couple of years ago. It's nothing though. Quadruple bypass.

TOM. Well, are — are you okay?

JERRY. Of course I'm okay. Look, nowadays a bypass is like calling the plumber and getting your kitchen sink fixed. It's no big deal. *(Tom moves on, but Jerry stops him.)* She's lovely, Natalie. You make a great couple.

PROPERTY LIST

Liquor cabinet
Woman's silk scarf
Cell phone
1 heavy suitcase
2 lighter bags
Champagne
Silver Champagne ice bucket with ice
Champagne glasses
Tray with plate of 10 muffins
Small velvet ring box
Engagement ring
Coats for Tom, Nat and Marnie
Cognac bottle
Scrabble set
Washcloth
Water pitcher and glass
Cider
Key
Cigar box
Pistol

SOUND EFFECTS

Faint violin music
Cell phone ring
Pop of champagne cork
Gunshot
Applause

NEW PLAYS

★ **AFTER ASHLEY by Gina Gionfriddo.** A teenager is unwillingly thrust into the national spotlight when a family tragedy becomes talk-show fodder. "A work that virtually any audience would find accessible." –*NY Times.* "Deft characterization and caustic humor." –*NY Sun.* "A smart satirical drama." –*Variety.* [4M, 2W] ISBN: 978-0-8222-2099-2

★ **THE RUBY SUNRISE by Rinne Groff.** Twenty-five years after Ruby struggles to realize her dream of inventing the first television, her daughter faces similar battles of faith as she works to get Ruby's story told on network TV. "Measured and intelligent, optimistic yet clear-eyed." –*NY Magazine.* "Maintains an exciting sense of ingenuity." –*Village Voice.* "Sinuous theatrical flair." –*Broadway.com.* [3M, 4W] ISBN: 978-0-8222-2140-1

★ **MY NAME IS RACHEL CORRIE taken from the writings of Rachel Corrie, edited by Alan Rickman and Katharine Viner.** This solo piece tells the story of Rachel Corrie who was killed in Gaza by an Israeli bulldozer set to demolish a Palestinian home. "Heartbreaking urgency. An invigoratingly detailed portrait of a passionate idealist." –*NY Times.* "Deeply authentically human." –*USA Today.* "A stunning dramatization." –*CurtainUp.* [1W] ISBN: 978-0-8222-2222-4

★ **ALMOST, MAINE by John Cariani.** A cast of Mainers (or "Mainiacs" if you prefer) fall in and out of love in ways that only people who live in close proximity to wild moose can do. "A whimsical approach to the joys and perils of romance." –*NY Times.* "Sweet, poignant and witty." –*NY Daily News.* "John Cariani aims for the heart by way of the funny bone." –*Star-Ledger.* [2M, 2W] ISBN: 978-0-8222-2156-2

★ **Mitch Albom's TUESDAYS WITH MORRIE by Jeffrey Hatcher and Mitch Albom, based on the book by Mitch Albom.** The true story of Brandeis University professor Morrie Schwartz and his relationship with his student Mitch Albom. "A touching, life-affirming, deeply emotional drama." –*NY Daily News.* "You'll laugh. You'll cry." –*Variety.* "Moving and powerful." –*NY Post.* [2M] ISBN: 978-0-8222-2188-3

★ **DOG SEES GOD: CONFESSIONS OF A TEENAGE BLOCKHEAD by Bert V. Royal.** An abused pianist and a pyromaniac ex-girlfriend contribute to the teen-angst of America's most hapless kid. "A welcome antidote to the notion that the *Peanuts* gang provides merely American cuteness." –*NY Times.* "Hysterically funny." –*NY Post.* "The *Peanuts* kids have finally come out of their shells." –*Time Out.* [4M, 4W] ISBN: 978-0-8222-2152-4

DRAMATISTS PLAY SERVICE, INC.
440 Park Avenue South, New York, NY 10016 212-683-8960 Fax 212-213-1539
postmaster@dramatists.com www.dramatists.com

NEW PLAYS

★ **RABBIT HOLE by David Lindsay-Abaire.** Winner of the 2007 Pulitzer Prize. Becca and Howie Corbett have everything a couple could want until a life-shattering accident turns their world upside down. "An intensely emotional examination of grief, laced with wit." *–Variety.* "A transcendent and deeply affecting new play." *–Entertainment Weekly.* "Painstakingly beautiful." *–BackStage.* [2M, 3W] ISBN: 978-0-8222-2154-8

★ **DOUBT, A Parable by John Patrick Shanley.** Winner of the 2005 Pulitzer Prize and Tony Award. Sister Aloysius, a Bronx school principal, takes matters into her own hands when she suspects the young Father Flynn of improper relations with one of the male students. "All the elements come invigoratingly together like clockwork." *–Variety.* "Passionate, exquisite, important, engrossing." *–NY Newsday.* [1M, 3W] ISBN: 978-0-8222-2219-4

★ **THE PILLOWMAN by Martin McDonagh.** In an unnamed totalitarian state, an author of horrific children's stories discovers that someone has been making his stories come true. "A blindingly bright black comedy." *–NY Times.* "McDonagh's least forgiving, bravest play." *–Variety.* "Thoroughly startling and genuinely intimidating." *–Chicago Tribune.* [4M, 5 bit parts (2M, 1W, 1 boy, 1 girl)] ISBN: 978-0-8222-2100-5

★ **GREY GARDENS book by Doug Wright, music by Scott Frankel, lyrics by Michael Korie.** The hilarious and heartbreaking story of Big Edie and Little Edie Bouvier Beale, the eccentric aunt and cousin of Jacqueline Kennedy Onassis, once bright names on the social register who became East Hampton's most notorious recluses. "An experience no passionate theatergoer should miss." *–NY Times.* "A unique and unmissable musical." *–Rolling Stone.* [4M, 3W, 2 girls] ISBN: 978-0-8222-2181-4

★ **THE LITTLE DOG LAUGHED by Douglas Carter Beane.** Mitchell Green could make it big as the hot new leading man in Hollywood if Diane, his agent, could just keep him in the closet. "Devastatingly funny." *–NY Times.* "An out-and-out delight." *–NY Daily News.* "Full of wit and wisdom." *–NY Post.* [2M, 2W] ISBN: 978-0-8222-2226-2

★ **SHINING CITY by Conor McPherson.** A guilt-ridden man reaches out to a therapist after seeing the ghost of his recently deceased wife. "Haunting, inspired and glorious." *–NY Times.* "Simply breathtaking and astonishing." *–Time Out.* "A thoughtful, artful, absorbing new drama." *–Star-Ledger.* [3M, 1W] ISBN: 978-0-8222-2187-6

DRAMATISTS PLAY SERVICE, INC.
440 Park Avenue South, New York, NY 10016 212-683-8960 Fax 212-213-1539
postmaster@dramatists.com www.dramatists.com